FOR
PAULA CHAMBERS

WITH EVERY GOOD WISH
Harry B. Davis
JANUARY 1, 2002

In appreciation for
your mentoring and friendship,
I want you to have one
of my Dad's books. Thanks
for being such a wonderful
pastor and role model!
Love, Dawn

# SONGS

## *Along the Missouri*

BY

HARRY BENOIST DAVIS

THE LOWELL PRESS/KANSAS CITY, MISSOURI

FIRST EDITION
Copyright © 1981 by Harry Benoist Davis
Library of Congress Number 81-85985
ISBN 0-913504-74-2

*Printed in the United States of America*

# DEDICATION

*To Marvis Holt Davis, and our daughters
Dawn, Melody, Delight, Miracle, Heather,
and Heidi, and to Dawn's husband Robert
Linnabery and son Casey, and to Delight's
husband Craig Wise and children
Amber, Matthew and Christopher*

*and
a special dedication to
Reginald D. Woodcock,*

*patron of the Benoists, sponsor of this book,
and author of a biography of my mother's
brother, Thomas E. Benoist, founder
of aviation in St. Louis.*

# TABLE OF CONTENTS

# Table of Contents

# INTRODUCTION

*Songs Along the Missouri* began when I as a river village youth of seventeen wrote while under the spell of the great river flowing beneath the high undulating bluffs which formed the horizon of "The Emerald Valley," my home. "A Boy's Road," "The Throne of Rocks," and other pieces were preserved from this period. "Adventures Which Must Transcend Time," and the University poems were written when I was eighteen, with others following, though most of the collection was created in later years.

These early river poems were written in the Saint Charles County village of Defiance, Missouri, where I lived with my preacher father, Rev. David R. Davis; my mother, Martha Benoist; and their other children, David, Howard, Margaret (Owen), Martha (Ware), and Richard in 1932 and during the university years at Columbia, Missouri, 1933 to 1937. I taught in the Mount Zion Bible School at Ava, Missouri, and in the Kansas City College and Bible School, received an M.A. in teaching English at the University of Kansas City, 1944, and a Master's in Divinity at Garrett Theological, Northwestern University, which enriched the poetry as well as my life.

My lifetime has been spent teaching in religious and public schools, and ministering in the United Methodist Church. My late father, my brother Richard, his son Bruce, and I are all Methodist preachers, and my siblings are all church leaders. Some of the better poetry was composed during my ten years as minister of Kansas City's Aldersgate United Methodist Church while living on secluded Cambridge Street with Marvis and our six daughters. These are the Cambridge Street Poems.

For some years I have occasionally given poetry readings to Rotary, school, and club groups, and some have suggested the publication of the poems. Finally I have proposed after a lifetime of poetry to hand down to Marvis and to our daughters a select collection of poems preserved through the years and taken from a larger body of unpublished verse. I once wrote that

> One loved poem, discovered when we look,
> Justifies the existence of a book,

and if this be true, may some find here that which will justify the existence of *Songs Along the Missouri.*

HARRY BENOIST DAVIS

## THE FIRST POEMS

This book begins with the thoughts of a youth as he wandered along the roads that go along the wide Missouri and entertained the long thoughts a boy thinks, about the wonder of it all. He found songs to match the brakes and the willows and the turbulence beyond the water's edge, the love, the birds of blue and of red-winged black and time and the waters.

These poems are a part of the story of the river itself and are preserved in order that the lives lived in the valleys along which the waters flow might not be lost in the forgottenness as the bluffs are lost in the mist.

"Proclaim the Glad Tidings" is a tribute to the author's preacher father, David R. Davis, whose presence was an anchor of the boy's life, and the poem exalts the message the father proclaimed to the people who came to hear him in the Saint Charles County churches he served, the nearest being Pleasant Hill Methodist at Defiance. This poem was attached to the father's obituary in the Methodist Conference Journal in 1963, and bears the imagery of the country around "the bluff mass" and the river.

"A Boy's Road" celebrates the road which connects Defiance with Matson, which is two miles upstream from its sister village. The road is parallel with the river but some distance away. Looking southeast from this road across the two-mile-wide Darst Bottoms one sees the St. Louis County bluffs across the river, mentioned in the last lines of the poem. The youthful writer walked this road frequently to share some news or thoughts with his teen-age friend, Walter Groenemann. The towns were in the foothills rising out of "these bottom lands," on the north side of the valley.

"The Throne of Rocks" was a place at the west edge of Defiance where the Francis Howell High School senior meditated. It was formed by some low rocks overlooking the wheat land and pecan groves of the valley, beyond which a wilderness of willows hid the river from sight, but from these rocks one saw the bluffs rising above the trees and the unseen river. The highest point of the bluffs was the middle one of three peaks, which like symbols of the Holy Trinity dominated the valley. This central peak was the "great rugged monument."

"Rural Autumn," composed in later life, was written on an outdoor table behind the Cambridge Street home in Kansas City, but carried the rural color of the riverlands. As October leaves rained down upon the table where the writer worked, he put the thoughts of fall on paper. The scenery of this piece reflects the farm where Marvis was reared. Ora and Dessie Holt reared their children, Calvin, Marvis, Justin, Kermit, and Erma, on a picturesque farm north of Galt, Missouri, and the farm scenes in this poem are those of their barns and home. Marvis, a Kirksville State University graduate, taught fourth grade at Bethany, Missouri, when she and Harry were married in 1955. The sometimes wind-rocked home of the Holts crowned a hill and was surrounded by cedars.

"On Leaving Home for the University" is mentioned in a story by the author called "The Emerald Valley," containing this passage:

> The last Sunday at home before the university was to open the next day, was a memorable one for Harry. . . .

> On this afternoon which he knew was to be his last at home, Harry stood before the old German church thinking of these things. He felt impelled to write. A stray piece of brown wrapping paper lay on the church lawn and he picked it up, then sat upon the lawn in front of the church, looking out across the river, and wrote on the brown paper his poem entitled "On Leaving Home for the University."

The church was the German Evangelical Church at Defiance where most of the German families attended, including his friend, Walter.

# SONGS
## Along the Missouri

*Missouri River, St. Charles County*    David Davis photo

## PROCLAIM THE GLAD TIDINGS

Proclaim the glad tidings that God in his pity
Makes known his great presence wherever man yields!
Good news in the village, sweet joy in the city,
Bright light on the mountains, and songs in the fields!

## A BOY'S ROAD

There is a winding road somewhere,
A town on either end;
My home is here, and you'll find there
My closest boyhood friend.
Beyond these bottom lands there flows
Missouri's roaring tide,
And towered above her banks there grows
The bluff mass at her side.

## THE THRONE OF ROCKS

From on my throne of rocks I view
The bluffs that rise to the endless blue
From the river Missouri's banks.
For a moment I make them a monument
To a love as full as the firmament,
And from here I return my thanks.

## THE BLUE MIST IS FILLING THE VALLEY TONIGHT

Written when the author was twenty, "The Blue Mist" preserves
the symbolic sacredness of the Emerald Valley.

Leaving the family of the Davises inside the lighted frame
parsonage at Defiance one June night, the poet walked out into the
backyard, looked across the Missouri at the mist-shrouded hills
beyond, and preserved the spell of their beauty in these lines.

## THE BLUE MIST IS FILLING THE VALLEY TONIGHT

The blue mist is filling the valley tonight,
The hills are all silent in haze,
And my heart looking up to the faltering light
Is deep with the fullness of praise.

I rejoice in the ways of both good men and saints,
The pathway where innocence flowers,
Where the joy of our God is the balm of complaints
And answered petitions are ours.

And I pray that the angels may stand soft above
The beds where some precious ones sleep,
That their breathings may kiss the sweet features I love,
Their wings guard the peace of the deep.

Let the mist cover up all I see in the vale,
No mist may envelope my hopes,
For a sacredness haunts me and love in the dale
Rolls deep on its forested slopes.

## RURAL AUTUMN

Hold back, hold back, you flowing winds of time,
Too swift, too swift, the colors lose their prime
As bright October leaves which burn the sky
With crimson, gold, and scarlet soon shall fly
Before autumnal motion, wind and breeze,
And lie in scattered heaps beneath the trees.
One gladdened with a red oak's deep maroon
Must feel some pain to know that all too soon
This rich mysterious foliage shall be found
Below benuded branches on the ground.
Blow wild, blow wild, you winds of autumn blow!

4

## Rural Autumn

Rain leaves, whirl leaves in one majestic show!
Be gone, be gone, the last of summer's breath
And blow the flowers their first foretaste of death.
Make haste and bring the fruits of harvest in.
Creak, wagons, hauling grain into the bin.
Let be cleaned out and strawed the sheds where sleep
On winter nights the huddled flocks of sheep,
The lordly rams and all their docile ewes
That in chill spring their lambs they may not lose.
The young fowls which once stretched out in the sun
And grew strong wings out in the pasture run,
Let be housed now from storms, enclosed in pens
To scratch beneath their straw-lined nests as hens,
While we within our wind-rocked homes defy
The face-benumbing blizzards of the sky.

Delight Davis-Wise photo

*The Holt farm in Galt, Missouri, scene of "Rural Autumn"*

5

# TIME AND THE RIVER

Out of the north flows the river mysteriously,
Out from the source of the dragon-like storms,
Out of the fogs and the mist lands imperiously,
Roaring, or noiseless through prairie land farms.

Often the herders of sheep in the pasture lands
Pause to behold on a lowering sky
Watery sheets closing in on the valley sands
Drenching them all as a storm races by.

Eastward pursuing its course gravitational
Onward the river traverses the state
Named for and naming the stream inspirational,
Blending the charm they together create.

Splendid in springtime are sights which the river land
Gives to the child who, along by the shore,
Walks with bare feet in the cool-feeling river sand
Lifting charmed eyes to the gray bluffs before.

Pleasant in summer the willows adjacently
Murmur through leaves adding joy to the swirl
Of the gliding Missouri whose waters complacently
Delight a vacationing youth and a girl.

High on the bluffs after oaks suffer autumn-freeze,
Across-stream they cast a red show to enthrall
Parents exploring with children for hickory trees,
Walnuts or bittersweet, ripe in the fall.

When comes the winter and valleys are blanketed
White with the snow, and with ice in the stream,
Those who are aging and white crowned hear
    trumpeted—
Time and the river are parts of one dream.

## ADVENTURES THAT MUST TRANSCEND TIME

Adventures that must transcend time
Are best preserved expressed in rhyme,
And yesterday, not far away
I went to see Augusta play
    Our Matson team.
You stood with bat in hand as I
Came, watching sizzling balls go by,
And with that smile you greeted me
Who you alone had come to see
    Or it would seem!
You had a pleasant day at bat,
Five hundred batted, for all that,
But on the field our shortstop keen
Was over, under, or between
    Most balls that came.
You were not feeling at your best;
What should be fun became a test.
Dull, slow, and tired you seemed to me
But then, when worst, you'll ever be
    To me the same.
I sat beside you on the ground
With known and unknown all around,
And joyed to have your teammates near
For nothing is to youth more dear
    Than having friends.
Angelic are the ties that bind
Admiring comrades of the mind,
And strong the loyalty of youth
And rich the search for life and truth
    Which never ends.

7

## ON LEAVING HOME FOR THE UNIVERSITY

Dear Lord, this vale of thine transcends
In beauty all the lands of old,
For on its crest Thy soul descends;
I see it in the tints of gold
That fade at evening from the hills;
I sense it on the scented breeze;
I hear it when the whippoorwills
Call from the darkened world of trees.

When from the hill's crest I perceive
The emerald valley set below,
With tears recall that soon I leave
Its haunts now fading with the glow
Of setting sun, then must my heart
Out of its very depths compose
A prayer for those from whom I part,
O keep them safe in love's repose.

## AFTER A VACATION FROM THE UNIVERSITY

That Sunday when I had to part
And leave my home behind,
The day was cold, the time was short
But you came to my mind.
I walked out through the misty air
On gravel wet and new;
I could not leave that place so fair
Without a word with you.
A cherished friend you are to me
And friendship has no end,
And I to you will ever be
No ordinary friend.

8

No damp and misty, dreary day,
No wind that ever blew
Could keep me from down Matson way
To say goodbye to you!

## LILACS

In the year 1915 the Reverend David R. Davis was the minister in charge of the Methodist church at Potosi, Missouri. On Sunday morning, May 2, he preached his sermon in the church building which until recently housed the Methodists of Potosi, then hastened home to the large two-story frame parsonage which housed the preacher there, and checked on Martha Benoist Davis, his wife.

About 3:00 p.m., the author of "Songs Along the Missouri" was born. The physician who lived near the Davises had been hastily summoned and the event went off without incident. The first kiss which the baby received was from the Negro maid.

This poem shifts scenery to a home just south and west of St. James where the family lived in 1929, and "where in a lilac yard a boy enjoyed a woodland farm."

May second is my day of birth,
A time when here and there on earth
The lilacs are in bloom.
How happy when each blue grenade
Explodes in bloom, and if it fade
There is a touch of gloom.

Some lilac bushes used to be
Behind the farmstead home where we
Once lived outside St. James,
And on my fourteenth birthday they
Provided background for our play
Like Moses' bush in flames.

A generation with its years
Has passed us by since we with tears
Were taken from the charm

9

Which we had known through months of joy
Where in a lilac yard a boy
Enjoyed a woodland farm.

Yet through the years I still recall
The times when lilac bushes all
Brought forth their purple mirth,
As in that legendary May
When Mother brought the second day
A Sunday boy to birth.

## UPON THE HILLS OF HOME

Upon the hills of home this Christmas night
The moonlight falls and lights the deep-piled snow,
As cold and real on valleys still as white
As in the days we knew so long ago.

The sky of twinkling miracle and light
Whose coursing stars once held a brighter flame
As angel choirs first sang one winter's night
High over Bethlehem, is still the same.

And in the homes of men who once were boys
Whose youthful faces wore the yuletide glow
One still may from their children hear the noise
Their fathers made long Christmases ago.

And thou, great Father of our wistful hearts,
We all would as thy children have a place
Where in thy kingdom we could take our parts
And as the pure in heart could see thy face.

O holy hope of all our lonely dreaming,
We have no words to tell thee how we long

10

To know the secret of the starlight streaming
Upon the vision of the angels' song.

And thou who hast this longing deeply written
Upon the inner chambers of the soul,
Let us be for our blindness keenly smitten,
And by thy healing kindness be made whole.

Then as this Christmas season's passing flight
Is gone, as are the homes of other days,
We would retain forever all the light
Of Christmas kindness, love and grateful praise.

## PARADOX

The infinite, to play an infant's part
Was born a child inside a barn for me,
But unless I find Christmas in my heart
I'll hardly find it underneath a tree.

## SHEPHERDS

Out on the bare, cold ground the shepherds lay
And did not know that the departing day
Would count upon earth's calendars the last
Before one era dawned, and one was passed.

They did not guess the watch they had to keep
Out on the hillside guarding flocks of sheep
Would soon erupt into a dazzling song
Conducted by archangels with a throng:

"Glory to God in the highest! On earth
Peace and good will be with men at his birth!
Praise God in the heavens; praise him in the height;
Praise, sun and moon and all you stars of light!"

The angels passed, the singing dying down,
The shepherds passed, on to the sleeping town,
The search for God passed to an infant's face;
Then passed my sins, for he was in my place!

## APRIL RAINS

April rains, April rains, steady the downpour!
April rains, refreshing the world!
Miracles descending, bring with them gladness,
Share with us pleasure as we in the downpour
Wade shoeless the culvert at road edge,
Wet bare feet, primitive, enjoying
The rivulets through toes and over ankles
Steadily flowing. April rains, April rains!
There shall be food; there shall be flowers;
There shall be pasture. The colt kicks
High in the bluegrass. The cow gives
Nourishment for her calf and for us.
Women in cities glean in the stores.
Babies chortle in young loving arms.
The legs of the athlete bulging with strength
Soar high over bars, race swift on the turf.
Scholars, legislators, toilers, and presidents
All are sustained by the thriving terrain
Hailing the rains, the April rains,
All perfect gifts from the Father of lights
And the Father of love and of life and of food
And of April rains, April rains, April rains!

*Site of "Swope Park at Snowtime"*

## LINES IN SWOPE PARK AT SNOWTIME

Wild winter whiteness, covering the park,
Stay hard, freeze hard, for soon it will be dark
And bitter cold will then preserve the awe
Of your pure whiteness from the threat of thaw.
Would we could crush forever to our hearts
This beauty, or preserve it through the arts,
That this horizon clad in crystal trees
And diamond covered branches we could freeze
And could possess together in some hold
Where summer heat could not destroy the cold.
But since this is impossible, at least
Let us look long upon the fields and feast,
Lest we should in reflection and repose
Lose ever this white treasure of the snows.

13

## WHOM HAVE I ON EARTH BESIDE THEE

Jesus, in human history
No other can be found
Who owns completely all of me
My source, my spring, my ground.

Yours are these hands, these arms, these feet
Yours are this face and heart;
Yours are these knees, with prayers, complete
With every human part.

Mine is the bleeding brow once lowered,
The thorn-crowned, sacred head
On which the spikenard once was poured
Which Mary richly spread.

Mine are the feet she bathed with tears
Which with her hair she dried,
Feet to be torn with nails while jeers
Deafened the crucified.

Mine is the love which there forgave
Us all who drove the nails,
And yours this life until the grave
Its tenure here assails.

## LION OF JUDAH

As a little boy I heard the deep thunder
Heard it from the pulpit at Eureka
In the peaceful outskirts of St. Louis,
With the red-robed Christ in the window behind
Lending the sermon celestial enforcement,
Calling as a mighty lion to its young.
Out of Zion the voice of the Lord
Roared as the voice of a conquering lion

And I heard his call from my luminous pew
And forward I went to the altar kneeling,
Not once, not twice, but often returning
As the conquering lion of the tribe of Judah
Roared to its young, and the young lion heard.
Then I came to the voice of the roaring
And lent my voice to the mighty waters
And lent the young lion's roar to his elder's,
Took up the calling, renewing the voice
That to the generation around me
There might never be lack of the thunder,
That with the departure of him, my father,
Voice of the Lord to his people calling,
I the younger should see that from Zion,
Sounding to those of my nation hearing
Should be the roar of the word of the Lord.

## BEFORE MEN WALKED ON THE MOON

The thought of travel to the stars brought man
To instruments of science for the quest
Of outer space, and missiles seemed the best,
Most logical provision for his plan.
At last a rocket stood against the dusk
Above an arc-lit launching pad at night,
Awaiting morning's count down time for flight
And for its Herculean starward thrust.
Man in successive stages since has flown
Vast orbits in the spaces and shall soon,
When all his plans to readiness have grown,
Place flags and human feet upon the moon.
We also wait the hour when he shall find
Like means to speed the healing of mankind.

## THE ROCKET

There looms outlined above the cape at dusk
A bold and gleaming missile and the light
That still remains reveals the fevered, brusque,
And hurried preparations of a flight.
The rocket stands there like the naked tusk
A massive beast thrusts through the jungle night,
Or like a corn ear shucking off its husk
To be the seed for fields beyond its sight.
Erect it stands, a symbol of man's bent
To challenge time and pass its limits by,
Aimed like a mighty bullet to be sent
To pierce the spheres whose portals man would try,
Or like some giant phallus, poised intent
Upon the impregnation of the sky.

## WALK ON THE MOON

Tonight I look up at a crescent moon
Glimmering golden in the sky of night
And know that men from earth this afternoon
Have landed there, and their astonished sight
Takes in what other eyes have never seen.
They breathe their thanks where no one ever knelt.
On territory silent and serene
They walk a surface no feet ever felt.
Walk on the moon, you men of earth, walk on,
Clad in your bulky, hooded whiteness, walk,
And leave your plaque upon its pitted lawn,
And plant your flag upon those fields of chalk!
For until now in all of time's vast span,
No walk like this was ever made by man.

16

## GREAT DIPPER CIRCLING ROUND THE NORTHERN STAR

Great dipper, circling round the northern star,
A magnetism holds you in its thrall.
You cannot deviate and cannot fall
Within your vast immensities afar.
Once Cheops from his pyramidal base
And Ramses, later, saw your course with awe,
While Homer glimpsed within the cosmic law
Achilles circling Troy in Hector's chase.
The Buddha thought you chained within a wheel,
And Jesus heard with joy your endless song.
Through glasses Galileo saw the reel
Of one revolving world amid a throng.
And I, beside this midland stream can feel
The timelessness of right pursuing wrong.

## SONNET: FARTHER ON

On, farther on, explorers of the west
Pushed with their wagon trains, intent to prod
Into rich nature's undisclosed facade
And be where none before had ever pressed.
Courageous faith led many to invest
Their fortunes as adventure's beckoning nod
Enticed them on to toil in virgin sod
And to rejoice in cabins they possessed.
When possibilities on land were spent,
Disdaining Alexander's tears their eyes
Perused the heavens and their cunning sent
Bold rockets into space to test the skies.
Now other worlds are waiting on man's bent
To pierce the space which spirit occupies.

17

## SAINT JAMES

Saint James is but a town upon the way
One travels from Saint Louis to the heart
Of Ozark lands where men and mountains play,
Yet still because I one time was a part
Of her calm village life I now can see
The scenes through which the feet of boyhood brought
Me often and which still in reverie
Compose a setting for adulthood thought.
That wintry day in March of 'Twenty-nine
Still seems as yesterday when, with the sun,
We rose in Licking, and with its decline
We saw our life in our new home begun.
The heavy-laden truck with all our things
Piled high, including treasures from the past
Moved on its northward way with creaking springs
Until it reached our farmstead home at last.
There we unloaded every chair and bed,
A bookcase I had built on Licking lawn,
A crate of Barred Rock hens—with two crushed dead,
The furniture and rugs we lounged upon.
Adventure's lure, which every child enthralls
Impelled us to explore without delay
The path down to the barn where, from the stalls
We climbed the rungs that led up to the hay.
From this enchanted loft out to the west
We looked down on a high-fenced garden site
With other buildings at the ends, and best
Of all, a tree-lined pond upon the right.
Off to the left and out beyond this scene
Our house stood on a wooded eminence
And we could see its rearward walls between
The oaks that towered above the garden fence.

## BERRY PICKING

Pail in hand descending
Rock strewn pathways ending
Where the woods are blending
With the pasture land,
Children picking berries
Find a patch that varies,
Fill a pail that carries
All they find at hand.

## BOYS AND FARM TASKS

Out the back gate flew they
Where the Rock chicks grew they
And the egg hens knew they
And all the world was fair!
Here the milk cows fed they
Put the ducks to bed they
Then to supper sped they
For joy was everywhere!

## AMOS

The shepherd, Amos, standing at Tekoa
On clear days saw the distant walls of Zion.
Forgotten were the python and the boa
As was the chilling roaring of the lion.
Absorbed he stood and through the thin air sought
To capture what details he could discern
Of Zion, dwelling place of God, and thought
Of Yahweh's cause, man's ultimate concern.

The limestone boulders in the wilderness,
The jagged cliffs, the broken paths of rock,
Contrasted with the manly tenderness
With which he tended his imperiled flock.
His ear had heard the paralyzing roar
Which told his shepherd ear a sheep was slain,
And he would find as he had found before,
A lamb's red blood upon some tawny mane.

But like one who would come and say (whose birth
Would be at Bethlehem eight centuries hence):
"Fear not, small flock, you are of greater worth
Than many sheep," he thought of man's defense.

He loaded up his asses from the stacks
Of wool he clipped from sheep which he had grazed,
Then put his second crop upon their backs,
The fig-like fruit of sycamores he raised.
He, trekking northward, sought to find a door
At Bethel in whose wide bazaars he sold
His figs and wool to feed and clothe the poor,
And for them got his small return of gold.

He watched the traders trap the poor in debt
And have their victims sold as slaves, for toil,
Looked on with wary eyes as the inept
Lost through false weights the products of the soil.
Upon his ears the songs and harps at feasts
Rang out to lure men to the sacred court
To lie with temple prostitutes, that priests,
Through compromise, might profit from the sport.

20

He saw the needy crushed, and with disdain
The righteous sold for silver, and the spurned
Sold for a pair of shoes, and infants slain
As sacrifices which their parents burned.

He seethed as devotees of Moloch filed
Before the idol in whose sides of fire
A furnace roared, and cast each first-born child
Into its arms to scream and to expire.

Then stood intrepid Amos in the road;
The passion of his God welled up within.
No force could have restrained the mighty load
Of Yahweh's blazing anger at their sin.
Upon an elevation in the street,
The place unmarked by centuries gone by,
He stood with homespun clothes and dusty feet
Which half concealed the purpose in his eye.

He lifted up his voice before the throng
That milled around the temple close at hand,
His fear of man submerged before the wrong
Inflicted on the poor across the land.
His voice became a trumpet as he bore
The wrath which gave him power to overwhelm,
And Bethel heard the Lion of Judah's roar
Come thundering across the northern realm.

"Your feast days and assemblies I despise!
I will not smell the incense which you wave!
Your burning meat is evil in my eyes!
Your sacrifices have no power to save!

Because Damascus threshed in Gilead
With threshing instruments of iron, my wrath
Shall far exceed that in the Iliad
Or Sampson's with an ass's jaw in Gath!

Because the cries of helpless captives rose
From those enslaved by Gaza and by Tyre,
And since they showed no pity to their foes
Their palaces shall be destroyed by fire!
In vain you seek the day of Israel's Lord!
That day is darkness and it is not light,
As if one fled a lion and rushed toward
A bear which stopped and mauled him in his flight!
Your harps and singing nauseate my soul,
For what you are is not that which you seem;
Like cloudbursts on the land, let justice roll,
And righteousness flow like a mighty stream!"
These things the prophet Amos spoke, and turned
To leave the spot where he had thrust the sword
Of God into men's souls as Bethel burned
With anger and repentance at his word.

Some twenty-seven centuries have rolled
Across the planet earth since Amos passed
And left foundations on which man can mold
The only revolution that will last.

## LOVE IS A GLOW

Love is a glow of never failing light
Surrounding every head.
Love is a father standing in the night
Beside his children's bed.

22

Love is communion keeping wedded life
As sweet as it began.
Love is the tender pity which a wife
Has for a struggling man.
Love was the cry which from our spirits rose
When those we loved were gone.
Love is the yearning which we have for those
Who beautified the dawn.
Love is the prize which is the goal of strife
When struggles all have ceased.
Love is the beautiful repast of life,
Its everlasting feast.

## THE PRAYER OF A PREACHER

From the period in which the writer began his career as a minister, while still following that of a teacher, the roles of servant of the church and poet crossed to produce this prayer.

Its discovery around 1945 by the father of the poet resulted in its being printed on pink cards at the Breckenridge, Missouri newspaper office by the father, Reverend D. R. Davis, who mailed a copy to his surprised son, the author, in Evanston, Illinois, where he was in Garrett Theological Seminary.

Soon shall the time for preaching overtake me,
Hearts that I love before my face I'll see;
O that some shock eternal might awake me,
Cause me to preach as one who speaks for thee!
I cannot bless unless at first thy blessing
Comfort and warm this barren breast of mine.
Men cannot come eternal life possessing
If thy poor branch be severed from the vine.

23

This face, dear Lord, let be both kind and tender,
This voice, dear Christ, an unction let pervade,
Lest I, thy servant, being seen, might hinder
Some heart from finding, or might one dissuade.
O thou transfigured, Christ-like God, our Father
Thou King of kings, omnipotent, behold
The church and give it power to gather
The scattered sheep and bring them to the fold.

## THE LINCOLN RESIDENCE

Upon a Springfield corner sweltering
In August heat our family stood and mused
Upon the weathered dwelling sheltering
The quaint possessions which a great man used.

We stepped into the Lincoln residence,
Inside of which we waited long to be,
And there saw treasures in full evidence
Which justified the wait in line to see.

A hall tree bore a shining stovepipe hat
Resembling one a century before
Which one had hung there with an old cravat
No longer needed once inside the door.

Then from the hall just to the left we stepped
Into the right front room to which it led
And saw the coarse black lounge where once had wept
A stricken father when his boy lay dead.

We journeyed clockwise through the rooms downstairs
Past chairs, and desks, and tables where he dined;
A sculpture of his hand lay near the wares
Upon which the original reclined.

## The Lincoln Residence

We saw the children's playthings and a chest,
A wicker chair and toys strewn on the floor,
As if the decades had not dared molest
The furnishings so treasured years before.

We climbed the stairs which once his tiring feet
Ascended, seeking rest when overtaxed,
Where he found waiting, with the day complete
The high four-poster on which he relaxed.

Adjacent to his bed a desk and chair
Stood silent, waiting, that when he awoke,
Should he possess some inspiration there,
He might transcribe his thoughts before he spoke.

Here at his desk he first sought to express
His thoughts in sentences replete with charm
Long years before the Gettysburg Address
Breathed its profundity of thought and form.

Descending by a staircase in the rear
We saw the hearth with pans for eggs and buns,
Where breakfast waited till he would appear
To sit at table with his wife and sons.

We took our leave of this historic place
Where that vast figure once had lived and talked,
And as we left the scene a brooding face
Filled our imaginations as we walked.

# THE WHITE SNOW IS FILLING THE VALLEY TODAY
## (WINTER 1966)

Here the writer as a family man watches the snow envelop the homesite as five little daughters frolic on sleds downhill behind their Kansas City home at 5017 Cambridge Street. Behind the house lay a valley in the midst of the city comprised of seventy acres of undeveloped woodlands in which the family made garden and kept their show bantams, the cochins, games, and others.

As the snow filled the unspoiled wooded valley in West Missouri which was his home as a man, he watched it one morning, and paraphrased the words which he had applied one night to a valley in Eastern Missouri which was his home as a youth, when he wrote "The Blue Mist Is Filling the Valley Tonight."

The white snow is filling the valley today
The flakes coming thick as a cloud,
And dim is the light as the white Milky Way
Envelopes us all like a shroud.

Though we older ones think of the penalties brought
By the ice in the yard and the street,
It is all sheer delight to the child who is caught
By the magic of snowfall and sleet.

Snowy Dawn and Delight and sweet Melody slide,
Downhill Heather and Miracle sleigh,
As their mother stands watching them snugly inside
From her window and sees them at play.

Snow is joy, youth is glad, and the winter can bring
Icy joys they can only have now,
For the snow will be gone with the coming of spring
When the buds blossom bright on the bough.

*Aldersgate parsonage, scene of "The White Snow"*

## OLD FRIENDSHIPS ARE LIKE SHIPS

Our friendship's long been at an end;
I don't want to renew it,
But sweet it is to meet again
Since we have both been through it.

My life's arranged as I would choose
Though you're no longer in it,
And reacquaintance would confuse
Our minds if we could win it.

Old friendships are like ships which speck
The sea, and drawing near them,
We catch the voices on the deck
Which pain us as we hear them.

So just a glimpse and then farewell,
And glad it happened to us.
We must not tarry lest the spell
Should threaten to undo us.

27

Our friendship's long been at an end;
We just must not renew it,
But sweet it is to meet again
Since we have both been through it.

## LOST LOVES

O where do lost loves go?
To where do they retire?
What winds snuff out their glow?
What waters quench their fire?

They must not wholly die
For memory retains
The vestige of a sigh
Above their sad remains.

The one who once has cared
Cannot undo the groove
Which once he neatly pared
Upon the desk of love.

O where do lost loves go?
To where do they retire?
What winds snuff out their glow?
What waters quench their fire?

## OUR GOD

You are our joy at dawn, O Lord,
Within your people's hearts adored,
And through the daylight hours, the strength,
Sustaining labor through their length.
You are our glory when the shade
Of evening covers all we've made,
And you the source through failing light
Of sweetest songs throughout the night.

## CHRISTMAS JOURNEY

On Christmas with the children bundled warm
We drove up north with visions of the food
Grandmother had awaiting at the farm
Whereon their mother grew to womanhood.

Our Kansas City home on Cambridge Street
We left by Sni-A-Bar and by Blue Ridge,
Then where the freeway and Missouri meet
We paid our toll at the Paseo bridge.

We glanced down on the legendary stream
Whose cold December flood is little changed
From rural boyhood's recollected dream
Though seen now with the background rearranged.

Missouri's greatest tower, the Power and Light,
Its color-changing dome now stilled and gray,
Which after dark provides the city night
Its most esteemed electrical display.

The City Hall whose grand ascending shaft
Sweeps upward past the mayor's lofty nest
And forms a walkway in the winter's draft
Whose view of all the city's is the best,

The Court House which one sees across the street
Made famous by the song, "The Twelfth Street Rag,"
Where upper jail cells and cold courtrooms meet,
Where abject inmates feel the long days drag,

The two great buildings of the Telephone,
The old one's ghostly tower now just a part
Of a communicating system grown
Beyond the bounds it planned for at the start,

29

The new library building where the Board
of Education's architectural mask
Conceals an ancient literary hoard
To cast new light upon the current task,

And to the east of these the massive hulk,
The building which the federal government
Has thrown up with its monolithic bulk
Against an unbelieving firmament,

The Muehlebach in whose Presidential Suite
The Eisenhowers and Trumans found their rest,
And where the Kaw and the Missouri meet,
An airport flinging planes against the west,

The Auditorium whose games and bouts
Attract great throngs, which also forms the stage
Where culture, art, and pageants by the Scouts
With politics and circuses engage,

The high Fidelity, whose tall twin towers
Above the maze by roads and rivers crossed,
Whose clocks, so seldom right, suggest the hours
Which our swift-flowing lives so soon exhaust,

The Commerce Tower whose sheer illumined height
Embraces sky-high dining joys by day,
Or, viewed from Briarcliff, throws out on the night
A galaxy of light across the way,

All loomed above us hymning to the skies
Their giant concert wrought in steel and stone
As we drove northward toward the joy that lies
In cherished fellowship and love alone.

## Christmas Journey

Our children live inside the city's bounds,
Yet love their fond grandparents' welcome farm,
The Holt estate which holds within its grounds
Just north of Galt, a rich ancestral charm.

Though generations pass and cannot stay
And time sees city skylines even move,
Though new ones rise, all things shall pass away
Except mankind's remembrances of love.

*Kansas City skyline*

Craig Wise photo

## TOUCH

When out of touch with Heaven, men are sad,
Their paradise is lost, its joys forgot;
But those in touch bear witness and are glad
When men who lack a living faith are not.

## BENEVOLENT INTELLIGENCE

Benevolent intelligence looked down
Upon an aggregate in Galilee
Assembled on the mountainside to see
His face or touch the borders of his gown.
Drawn by his magnetism and renown,
The deaf, the lame, the bound refused to be
Kept from their hope to be healed or be free
By opposition or official frown.
His eyes discerned that not all came to find
In him the proof of love's validity,
That other eyes disdained the humble mind
Through haughty looks brimmed with cupidity.
He started as he saw a cross, in blind
Mankind's malevolent stupidity.

## THE BIRTH OF JESUS

Said Balam, "I shall see Him but not now;"
And cried, "I shall behold Him but not nigh;
But now and nigh are here to seal the vow;
This is the place, the child, the star, the sky."

## FUNERAL FRAGMENTS

Martha Benoist Davis, the poet's mother, was one in the train of great women whose dignity, discipline, and reverence lay behind all that is truly great in the nation.

She passed away at Chillicothe, Missouri, September 21, 1961. Her grieving husband seeing her youthful picture cried, "Oh, what a girl she was!" A son's wife returning from the funeral said, "In all my life I have never known anyone who was half as great as Mother Davis."

Her influence in the church and upon many ministers and leaders reached far beyond her clerical sons.

A score of bustling kitchens still belong
To memories shared by all your parsonage brood
In which you sanctified with cheerful song
The harsh vicissitudes of motherhood.

Dear sweet and blessed, sainted mother heart,
What words could we conceivably recruit
To half begin to write the thousandth part
Of our bereaved, awed hearts' hushed, sad tribute?

### I BELIEVE:

That any cause which must be maintained
At the cost of rendering human beings expendable,
    Is expendable!
That no cause which must be maintained
At the cost of human sacrifice,
    Is worthy of support!
That murder through the waging of aggressive war,
    Is the ultimate crime;
That estranged man in his blind self-centeredness,
    Is utterly tragic;

33

That self-will toward anything except the will of God
And the good of all,
    Is evil;
And concerning preventive war waged abroad,
That nothing on earth that has to be saved at
  a cost like this,
    Is worth the saving.

## HEAD RESIDENT: INSTITUTIONAL CHURCH

At Institutional, the downtown church,
Was housed the Center for the neighborhood,
Staffed by devoted women in the search,
As deaconesses, for the common good.

Head Resident was saintly Dorothy Dodd,
Frail, slender, wraithlike, and a gracious host,
The nearest thing in womanhood to God,
Or, clad in dresses, to the Holy Ghost.

*The Author-Pastor at Institutional Church, 1944*

34

## A BALLAD OF BIRTHS

David R. Davis and his wife,
Martha Benoist, began their life
In nineteen-seven when they wed
And lived where his profession led.

From Mineral Point where they had loved
To Salem Circuit David moved
And there he brought his bride to live
Amid what comforts churches give.

DeSoto Circuit, nineteen-eight
Was home for David and his mate.
They moved in nineteen-nine to take
Steelville and Leasburg, and to make

Steelville their home, and there they spent
Two years which brought a great event
In nineteen-ten and with it, joy,
The birth of David, their first boy.

He reinforced them with his smile
And they took Hematite a while
In making still another search
To find a more appropriate church.

In nineteen-twelve they moved again
And in Saint James most bitter pain
Suspended on an infant's breath,
Descended with that infant's death.

Fair Elmer Glen made all days bright
For eighteen months, then passed from sight.
A nineteen-hundred-fifteen birth
Brought me in protest to the earth,

Potosi, the Missouri town
Where I, like eider, floated down.
In that same year, exchanging towns,
Our father took the church at Lowndes.

Whitewater where the grass looked green
Was home in nineteen-seventeen.
Whitewater shone like something bright
When brother Howard was born one night

In nineteen-eighteen just before
Desloge swung wide a welcome door.
Deslodge in nineteen-twenty blessed
Us with an infant in our nest,

The first of two girls, Margaret,
With long straight locks as black as jet.
That year I entered the first grade
One month before our father made

The move to Salem where a wee
Girl, Martha, joined the family.
We lived in Salem till that fall
Of nineteen-twenty-two when all

Migrated to another town,
Eureka, where we settled down.
The old church house beyond repair,
Our father built a new one there,

## A Ballad of Births

Then moved in nineteen-twenty-five
With two girls and three boys alive
And Mother, whose unvoiced complaint
Made her a much transplanted saint.

There in the Ozark hills he strove
To mold a life in Mountain Grove.
Insurance, for a time, he chose
To follow, seeking to compose

The fortunes of a family caught
In stringencies low salaries brought.
In Mother's room beneath the stair
One night a baby rent the air

With his first cry as overhead
We heard wee Richard from our bed.
In nineteen-twenty-six he came
To be the last to add his name
Completing all the births that fate
Might round the family out at eight.

The flood of time that ever flows
Has sorted things which stay, from those
Which upstream loomed large on the mind,
Yet in the sands are left behind.
The birth, the growth, the love, the strife
The elemental human life,
The fact of being, these hold fast
When less than human things have passed.

# THE PAGEANT OF THE PROPHETS

## Moses
"Today I've set before you life and death,"
Said Moses to the Jews. With his next breath,
"Choose life," he thundered and the mountains rang.
The unseen presences around him sang.
From him mankind had heard, above the waves
Of universal lostness, that which saves.

## Habakkuk
To hear some word from heaven for the race
Habakkuk on his watchtower took his place
And prayed some word would come to see the dearth
Of revelation lifted from the earth.
A thought like lightning flashed forth his reward:
"The just shall live by faith!" Thus spoke the Lord.

## Micah
"What shall I bring, to come before the Lord?"
The prophet Micah asked, "Come with a horde
Of rams, and yearling calves, or floods of oil,
Or burn my first-born? Come through blood and toil?
He only asks in every period,
Be just, be kind, and humbly walk with God!"

## Amos
Lone Amos stood like a Judean lion
And cried to all, "The Lord will roar from Zion,
'I hate your feasts; your conduct I despise,
Your burning meat is evil in my eyes!
Let justice roll like cloudbursts to redeem,
And righteousness flow like a mighty stream!' "

38

## THE MAN OF ALL CALLINGS

The Son of Man, called Jesus is called Christ,
Meaning anointed, and placed far above
All other names. He constitutes the theme
About which all religious men converse
When questions of theology are raised;
And likewise, those determined to rebel
Against the interferences which faith
Obtrudes upon their freedom, choose this One
To bear the brunt of their hostility.
Yet whether loved or hated, he is still
Contemporary with all serious minds
Which try to grapple with reality.
He is the perfect model which all men
Are measured by, and try to emulate.
Each sort of man finds him the perfect type
And symbol of perfection for his kind.
The farmer finds in him the Holy Ground,
Called the good soil on which all things subsist.
Likewise the sower knows him as the seed,
And to the traveler he is the path.
Vinedressers think of him as the true vine.
The florist calls him "Rose of Sharon,"and
"The lily of the valley,"too, is he.
The rancher knows his Heavenly Father owns
The cattle on a thousand rolling hills.
To herders with their flocks he is the good
Shepherd who lays his life down for his sheep.
The baker finds in him the living bread.
The butcher here beholds the helpless lamb.
To candlemakers he is the candle set
Upon a candlestick to light the world.

The laundryman holds him the only power
To blot stains otherwise indelible.
To tailors Jesus symbolizes robes
Of righteousness, the clothing of the saints.
Shoemakers find him shod that he might preach
Salvation's love (how beautiful the feet)!
The carpenter beholds in Nazareth
A carpenter apprenticed in his home.
The plumber sees in him the living spring
From which the waters of the Spirit flow.
In him stone masons strike the solid rock,
The architect finds him the cornerstone,
And engineers a highway and a way.
The greatest teacher, all who teach confess,
And businessmen find him the one with whom
The greatest business on earth is done.
The preacher finds him first of all who preach.
"The Great Physician," healers call this man.
The lawyer here beholds the "Advocate"
Who pleads with God the Father for our lives.
Here broken hearts have found a comforter.
No orator has spoken as has he.
Philosophers behold in him the truth,
And to historians he is the peak
Unrivalled in the history of the world.
The writer knows all rival themes are pale.
The poet saves for him his loftiest verse.
The artist paints his best for him alone,
And singers sing their most exalted song.
Composers here discover symphony.
One glorious face the beauty lover lures;
The prodigy beholds the twelve-year-old

Confound the elders in their temple seat,
And when matured his radiant person bore
Authority beyond the reach of kings.
The athlete finds in him the perfect man
Called the unblemished lamb and given a name
Upon whose vesture and upon whose thigh
The glorious name is written "King of kings."
Thus all mankind its greatest tribute brings
To the All Highest clothed in human form.

## SAMPSON AND THE LION

Strong Sampson loved a girl in Gath,
And in his wedding gown
Walked with his parents on the path
Descending to her town.

They passed a vineyard where they found
A grown young lion in wait
Which sprang, attacking with a bound
The bridegroom by the gate.

His flashing jaws were gripped by hands
So great in skill and brawn
That he was helpless as the bands
Of muscled arms stretched on.

The lion died as Sampson rent
And choked its life away,
And Sampson stood magnificent
Upon his wedding day.

## MISSOURI

From North Missouri's rolling hills which hold
A population agricultural
To South Missouri's Ozark ruggedness
With stalwart people matching its terrain,
A scenic part of the creation lies
Embracing this somewhat provincial
And isolated segment of the world.
So independent is it that a wall
Could be erected following the lines
That separate it from its sister states
Of mortar made with gleaming granite blocks
Mined from the Carthage quarries for the cause,
Tall as St. Louis built its Gateway Arch
Or as proud Kansas City's Power and Light
Whose massive walls of stone reach such a height
As causes rural youth who come to town
And bring their cattle to the Royal show
To gaze astonished at its pointed dome.

If such a wall enclosed the varied state
With culvert openings arched just enough
At the two northern corners of the state
To let the flowing Mississippi in
And to admit Missouri's rolling tide,
And yet another to the lower east
Allowing both to journey on their ways
Toward the southern gulf and distant seas,
Old sages say that all could live quite well
In total independence from the world
Because the state produces all the needs
Which elemental populations use.

42

However this may be, the mighty planes
That lift from Lambert Field upon the east
Or International upon the west
Preclude the possibility of walls.

Exporting men, from T. S. Eliot
To young George Washington Carver has been
For decades one Missouri industry
The world would be far poorer should it lack.
No wall could quite have held Mark Twain inside
For he, escaping from the lower gate,
Would with his Mississippi find a way
Out to a world to which he must belong.

The Allied Forces in the First World War
Could not have stormed to victory until
They first had stormed Missouri's wall to bring
The man, John Pershing, born inside Laclede
In North Missouri's central region, west
Of Mark Twain's place of birth at Florida,
To lead the Allied Armies of the world,
If such a wall had been erected there.

Between Laclede and Florida, but south
Of both, is Clark, Missouri, in which town
Was Omar Bradley born, who held command
Of all ground forces which the nation sent
Across the face of Europe in the war
Begun and lost by Germans in the thrall
Of moustached madness diabolical.

When the Atomic Age burst on the world
It was from hands Missourian unleashed
As from the White House came the fateful word
Which a Missouri president pronounced
As an impending sentence on mankind.

No wall could hold these forces from the world
Confined within their cradle where the streams
Which dominate the continent conjoin.
The meeting of the waters is enshrined
In statuary in St. Louis where
Beneath high Union Station's clock tower stands
The naked figure of a man with arms
Outstretched above a splashing fountain pool
Toward a lovely giant maiden, nude,
And reaching toward her longed-for lover's arms.
St. Louis with its Mississippi waits
For Kansas City's loved Missouri stream
That they, conjunct, might bind into one flood
Of union this vast gateway to the west.

The Gateway Arch which rises by the bridge
Which engineering genius, James Eads,
Both built and named, now rises to a height
Which relegates the former miracle
To an historic curiosity.

The old courthouse where Dred Scott's case was tried,
Which made its contribution to the swirl
Of controversy leading to the war,
Still stands historic near the gleaming arch.

*Kansas City skyline, Union Station in foreground*

Oblivious of history great crowds
Sometimes intent to watch world series play
Are packed inside the gleaming stadium
Whose high-tiered circular exterior wall
Now decorates the ancient water front.

Nearby the Old Cathedral still proclaims
The Changeless to the changing centuries,
Its dome erect and proud as if no arch
Had risen high to dwarf it in man's sight.
The New Cathedral in the city's midst
Holds lavish riches for both soul and art,
Though now itself bedwarfed by the DeVille,
The high adjacent motel to its west.
Yet arches and high rising luxuries
Must join cathedrals in high requiem
For all that is material on earth,
While lending cause with churches great and small
To the immortal spirit's enterprise.

Old Centenary Church which Methodists
From Carradine to Godbold utilized,
And grand St. John's, springboard of Bishop Holt,
Still stand in silent witness to the soul,
As do small unsung chapels spaced afar.

The pageantry of Being finds a voice
For living things, for animal and bird
In Forest Park whose zoological
Displays are scarcely equalled in the world.
The great gorilla pounding on his chest,
A dead one mounted, on display nearby,
Proclaim in life and death the mystery
Of animation and mortality.

The polar bear as white as fields of ice
Weaves his great form before admiring throngs
Surprised to find within our temperate zone
This grandeur from the distant arctic wastes.
The giant brown bear from Alaska stands
Upright, astounding all with unmatched size
Among meat-eating animals on earth.
Here love of humor finds a quaint delight
In the performance of chimpanzees which
Bicycle or enjoy a pony ride.

Beyond this maze of lion shows and sights,
The Gallery of Art, west in the park,
Affords a welcome quiet for a guest.
There Titian's "Ecce Homo" stands and bears
The witness of high innocence to those
Who plotted crucifixion on a hill,
A face in oils, surveying mankind's art,
The pageantry of culture it enriched.

46

## Missouri

The bronze St. Louis, mounted on his horse
Looks out upon the throngs the park attracts,
And wears his alternating coverings
Of intermittent heat and rain and steam,
Or, in midwinter, sheets of sleet and snow,
In witness that the monarch spirit braves
The elemental furies in its stride.

How fitting was it that when Lindberg flew
Alone, as if first on the moon, across
The vast expanse Atlantic, all alone,
"The Spirit of St. Louis"carried him
And came to rest in Paris which had sent
The Benoists to Missouri, decades past,
To foster aviation in the west.
North of St. Louis out on Kinlock Field
Tom Benoist flew his kite-like ship in air
Which he invented, times identical
With those who barely edged him from the fame
Of first inventing airplanes, when out east
The Wrights at Kitty Hawk flew first the craft
Which they and Benoist had conceived at once.
On Creve Coeur lake a craft with boats for wheels
And Benoist in the cockpit cleared the banks
And flying high above the horse-drawn flow
Of traffic saw St. Louis from the air.

He built the craft from which a parachute
First opened dropping mankind from a plane,
And at St. Petersburg in Florida
Established the first airline in the world
To carry mail and passengers aloft.

47

Cradle of aviation at its birth,
St. Louis was its hold in infancy,
And now at Lambert Field has come of age.

How little one who walks the city streets
Can see the ghosts of history arise
As, unaware, he occupies the points
Where in the same square feet of space once walked
Those whose names anchor history in place.
One traveling St. Louis streets may pass
Some place where with a wagon and a team
Ulysses Grant once trudged on foot to find
A buyer for the cord-wood he had hewn
From groves outside the city on his farm,
And farther on, along St. Charles roads
Out near Defiance in the northern hills
That rise from the Missouri, Daniel Boone
Discovered at long last, his final home.

Behind the hamlet, Matson, near a spring
He built his home which later he enlarged.
He drew his inspiration from the bluffs
Across the scenic river, rising high
In triple undulating peaks which stand
Like symbols of the Holy Trinity
Above the fertile bottom land he farmed.

With his son, Nathan, Daniel Boone then built
The strong stone mansion back among the hills
North of Defiance where one still may look
Up at the ceiling beams and see each slash
Made by the axe-head which he strongly swung,
The product of his strength when in his prime.

# Missouri

Here one may see the bedroom where he died,
And feel the legendary unity
That binds us to the heroes of the past.

Nearby St. Charles still contains the streets
Which lead to the first capitol which stands,
As it stood then, along a solid row
Of ancient storefronts in the oldest part
Of this old capitol where once the laws
Were made which governed an extensive state.

The seat of this state government was moved
A century and more ago upstream
To where Boone county's bluffs, seen bold across
The flood Missouri, stand like sentinels.
Here rose a gleaming dome, high over all,
Which still above its massive base of stone
Embraces the direction of a state
In this fair city named for Jefferson.

Strangers who wend their tourist ways along
The fertile slash which the Missouri makes
Between the cities where the great planes fuel,
Will find some gem-like towns, unvisited
By most, but which comprise great schools which teach
The midland young the lessons of the past.

Columbia, whose ivy-hidden walls
Are dominated by the spacious dome
Of Jesse Hall, and by red campus lawns,
Contains Missouri University
Whose six, tall, relic columns stand,
Stone symbols of a linkage to the past,

And are surrounded by a vast complex,
And by two other schools of much renown,
The fabled Stephen's College, school for girls,
And Christian College on its northern side.

The town, Fayette, on west, is still the seat
Of Central Methodist, pre-civil war
Established campus, and at Fulton, east,
Are two old colleges once visited
By Winston Churchill, who in Fulton gave
His famed Iron Curtain address to the world,
From Presbyterian Westminster's seat,
With William Woods, the girl's school, lying near.

Meanwhile the tide, Missouri, rolls its way
Along its bed toward its destined seas,
And symbolizing the eternal search,
Bears its rich witness to a distant home.

## INCIDENT AT A BOONVILLE BUS STOP

A Negro woman left a bus
Which made a Boonville stop
With a tiny girl whose restless fuss
Meant a rest room or a mop.
The rest rooms in the restaurant
Had printed signs which bore
The letters blacks feared to confront,
"White Only," on the door.

The manager saw her distress,
He saw the small child squirm,
But though he saw, would not digress,
But by his rule stood firm.
The small one could no longer wait,

# Incident at a Boonville Bus Stop

For as with food or thirst,
Some human answers come too late,
Some flooded dams must burst.

Humiliation and despair
May even clasp a child
When in soiled clothes which scent the air
And desperation wild
It stands a helpless victim of
Man's stupid lack of sense
When prejudice refuses love
To those without defense.

Among white passengers, one rose,
Wife of a minister,
Fired with a purpose to oppose
A thing this sinister.
"How do you dare in heaven's sight
Refuse a child who pleads
For that to which men have a right,
And which a small child needs?
Let this sad spectacle confound
Your attitude, and mend
The prejudice which here has found
You naked in the wind!"

The stunned proprietor stood sad
On being thus dressed down,
But worse than words he, too, had had
Some conflicts of his own.

He called each kitchen employee,
Each waitress, too, to come

Out to the scene that each might see
The child who stood there numb.

He looked upon them all and said,
"I've called you here to say
That our past policy is dead,
And shall be from this day.
I'm tearing down each wretched sign
Beneath both 'Hers' and 'His';
If anyone objects, resign—
For this is how it is!"

No one resigned as he tore down
The words and helped create
An atmosphere in Boonville town
Which brightened all the state.

## APRIL IN AUGUST

Hot winds of August, searing the summer,
Blow dry the grasses firing the gardens
Until comes the treasure, the late summer rain storm,
Fervently hoped for, awaited with longing,
Delayed in its coming until there is loss.
Vast are the losses when grain fields are burning,
But when come the rain waves sweeping the clover,
Soaking the corn fields, the stalks are revived.
In comes the coolness, relieving the fever
Of late summer weather, transforming the land.
Lovely is cloud cover bringing the downpour
And lovely the gain in the grain fields reviving.
We watch as the rainfall, steadily pouring,
Produces a cloudburst, the rarest of wonders,

*April in August*

April in August, the glory of summer,
For there shall be food and life is secure.
Blessed be summer and blessed be August,
And blessed be rainstorms and blessed be God!

## SCULPTURE OF THE RISEN CHRIST

In Santa Maria Sopra Minerva
In Rome stands one of the finest things known
To exemplify grandeur that man could observe
A majestic and glorious tribute in stone.

Enraptured, one gazing beholds the revealing
The risen Christ standing and holding his cross
In natural grandeur with nothing concealing
The grace of the figure which once bore our loss.

The great Michelangelo felt it his duty
Through human perfection alone to express
His highest rendition of spiritual beauty;
All else seemed but pretty, attractive, or less.

One fancies he sees him with chisel expanding
Some flawless detail which from rest has enticed
The rapt Michelangelo who almost seems standing
Beside his great crowning conception of Christ.

## CHRISTMAS 1975

The yule tree in our parlor glows
With many colored lights
And from the tree-stand, upward shows
Its eye-bedazzling sights,
Until when glancing at the top
We see an angel stand
In white so shining as to stop
Beholders with its wand.

Beneath the tree are packages
In brilliant wrappings dressed
To wait the day that manages
To sanctify the rest.
Our lives can never know decay
Nor we as Christians grieve
Who with the gifts on Christmas day
Its greatest Gift receive.

## MARTHA BENOIST

Around the year nineteen and five
As reckoned by the birth of Christ
(By whom all things, not time alone,
Are judged and will forever be)
A lovely girl, clad all in white
Walked up a creek bed toward a church,
Two other maidens also dressed
In white, her sisters, walking too
On Wallen Creek's hard pebbled path.
The Rock Creek church at streamside stood
Whose white frame walls had been put up
By farmers who desired a church.
Of these three pretty sisters, one,
Named Martha, caught the preacher's eye,
When he received and welcomed them,
Admiring her in innocence
For he was married at the time
And knew not death and destiny
Decreed their lives should interlace.
The girl at the piano for the hymns
Was Bessie Forshee, who would wed
A brother of the Benoist girls,
The one for whom I should be named
In future times, in future times.

## CREATIVITY

It's usually in an ivory tower
Or in the rare secluded hours
That writers summon up the power
Which creativity requires.
But here this morning in a room
I write while children play about,
And try to think while crash and boom
Resound to put my thoughts to rout.
They're mine. Six of them I begot,
Though not without their mother's say
And yet, five neighbors I did not,
Nor shall I sire much work today.

## CHRISTIANS AND SCIENCE

A little girl lay gasping for her breath
A deep pneumonia wearing out her heart
While her religious parents fought off death
With prayer, refusing medicine a part.

Practitioners of prayers for healing came
And used their affirmations for release,
But still no change within the heaving frame
Of breast still tortured by a grim disease.

The neighbors called police and summoned Health
Department intervention to provide
An ambulance and took her where a wealth
Of skilled hospital care was at her side.

There in Intensive Care she found relief
Who would have died had prayer alone been used,
But who can shrug and say that prayer in grief
Was futile for a family thus confused?

## NEW YEAR 1974

Today is the first day
Of nineteen seventy-four
The year in which I may
Improve things I deplore.

Procrastination's cost
Is hourly, yearly paid
In undone labors lost
And conquests never made.

If resolutions form
Within my wiser brain
I shall attempt to storm
Old castles once again.

## HYMN TO THE HEAVENLY SPIRIT

Heavenly Spirit, come refine
Your church that it may move,
That it may burst forth as a vine
Puts branches out to intertwine
In faith and hope and love.

Your call which makes our lives complete,
Above all wealth is priced.
How beautiful upon the street
And mountainside are still the feet
Of those proclaiming Christ.

A struggling church, a troubled race,
Are groping in the night.
Our unlit hearts, O set ablaze,
And let defeated souls amaze
Each other with their light.

A Holy Sonnet

## A HOLY SONNET

It seems a sweet and sacred thing to say
That one believes the Bible all the way
From front to back and entertains no doubt
That God could bring these miracles about.
But read in Joshua that God commands
The slaughter of all infants in those lands
And men and mothers put to death by sword
By Israelites in conquest for the Lord.
The question rises, could the God of Christ,
The Father of the Savior, be enticed
To make the land a conquest at the cost
Of death and terror from a conquering host?
O God, let not your love be sacrificed
Though biblical inerrancy be lost!

## THE NIXONS IN CHINA

I

Three quarters of a billion human minds
As earnest and concerned as any one
Of us in faraway America
Had for a generation kept a wall
Between them and the much-feared foreigner
So hostile to the state become their god.
Then from a giant plane flown from the east
Alighting from its flight out of the west
Emerged the chieftain from the other half
Of this swift-moving, round, revolving earth,
And at his side, the slender, fair, reserved
First Lady from the planet's western side.
This leader of the world, self-called "the free,"
Bore in his complex mind the huddled hopes

57

Of masses, mute, anonymous, and still,
Awaiting hopefully to hear the news
That some new aperture within the clouds
Might pierce the hostile storms that darken earth,
To crown this planetary episode.

## II

The President stepped from the grounded plane
In an experience as strange and new
As that first step man made upon the moon,
And, as man from the moon first saw the earth
As one round ball, the home of man in space,
And only one mankind on one round world,
This spokesman freshly from the other side
Of this world fractured by philosophy,
Stood where no president had ever stood,
American upon a Chinese land.

## III

Symbolic with him were two denizens
Of Arctic North America, flown in
To grace the Peking Zoo, a shaggy pair
Of mute Musk Oxen unknown in the East,
Brute pioneers caught in a circumstance
Bewildering to both their bovine brains,
So helpless in homesickness for their kind,
So helpful for an understanding world.

## IV

Beyond the shaking hands with Chou En-Lai,
Who welcomed both the Nixons and their train,
Were waiting banquets, beds, and scenery,
And views of the good earth, the sacred land,
Bedecked with snow, and trees and icy limbs,
And palaces now turned to monuments.

## V

In a gymnasium, the President
Sat with the Chinese Premier to view
Gymnastic feats performed by practiced youth
As Mrs. Nixon with high government
Officials of the highest privilege
Observed firsthand a spectacle of skill
And youthful beauty both of face and limb.
The powerful, muscled arms young Chinese men
Used to control their flights upon the swings,
The bare, curvaceous legs and graceful forms
Of Chinese girls performing on the bars,
Entranced the entourage and cast a spell
Of deep appreciation for the worth
And loveliness of this celestial land.

## VI

Two men sat long with their interpreters,
The President across from Chou En-Lai;
Each knew the other represented all
Which his own ideology opposed,
The one, with Christian training, Quaker style,
The other, atheist, without a god,
Materialist, believing in the state
As the supreme authority for man,
Yet in the other's eyes each recognized
The calculation of a brilliant mind.
Each had outrun his peers to lead his land,
And each possessed a genius defined
By his own ideology and goal.
Each previously had held so little hope
Of any common ground (on ground which one
Of them must feel cried to other one

For his brother's—millions of brothers'—blood)
As to produce an unbelieving awe
At speaking to each other face to face.
But an endangered planet with its hordes
Of human beings—billions in the quest
For some deliverance from atomic threat
Brought pressures from the human mass behind
To end the obscene race for armaments,
And blunt the insane power of overkill,
Of arming states to kill and maim mankind.

### VII

One hour the West's most celebrated man
Sat with the only god the Chinese know,
Or, are allowed officially to own,
The aging poet and philosopher,
The East's most famous man, Mao Tse-Tung,
The unifying father figure whose
Best selling works eclipse all other books
To mold the wistful, oriental mind.
It was significant that he who had
Inflamed his youthful followers to cast
With special zeal, all things American
To cultural revolutionary flames,
Now faced the incarnation of the things
He previously had launched his enmity
To imprecate, and found his foe his guest—
a guest whose quiet ways and friendly eyes
Disarmed his own and helped to heal a world.

### VIII

The aerial odyssey continued on
And Shanghai, famous to Americans,
Extended to the guests its open arms.

Here, and in other cities, visitors
Looked on an alien land much like their own,
Looked into children's eyes, dark and oblique,
Distinctly oriental, but the same
In loveliness as in America,
Saw faith and hope and love expressed in terms
Rich with the powerful longings of mankind.

IX

At last the great planes took their leave for home,
The journey done, for history to consign
The outcome to the judgment of the years,
But human confrontation, face to face,
Spirit to spirit, mind of man to mind,
Created some accord in kindliness
Which differs vastly from communiques
Impersonal and distant, bristling states
Would fling with arrogance and threats of force
Against the tender helplessness of man.

## O BLESSED FEET

O blessed feet and hands and face
Appearing long ago in space,
The body of our Lord!
Two thousand years have left no trace
So for our proof of time and place
Your presence is the word.

## EMILY DICKINSON

Emily Dickinson sought
Through poems, life to measure.
What a woman, what a thought,
What a poet, what a treasure!

*The Methodist Church, Slater, Missouri*

## NEW YEAR 1959, SLATER, MISSOURI, METHODIST CHURCH

Ring, bells of ancient belfrey holy,
Ring out and let all Slater know
That this new year, beginning slowly
With peals of bells across the snow
Is dedicated to the Lord!
Ring out to all, that we who preach
And we who hear shall strive to right
All things amiss, and toil to reach
Perfection in God's love, whose light
Shines through the everlasting Word.
Ring perfect love upon our town
And ring to man God's glory down!

## TO RICHARD IN FRANCE

The President, my dear, is dead
The German war is near its close
And destiny will soon disclose
The shape of things to greet or dread.

Then happy will reunion sound
Delirious news that battles cease,
That victory has bought release
From dire conflict the world around.

Dear brother, paratrooper, friend,
Your face we hope with joy to view
We trust we shall not weep for you
When war is done and shadows end.

We trust we do not pray in vain.
We only hope that life has led
You through the valley of the dead,
That we shall see your face again.

## SPIRIT

Every word that man has spoken
Gropes toward the Lord.
Every vow and promise broken
Loses some reward.

All the evil of man's madness
But augments the light.
Ways which but result in sadness
Testify of right.

Every act of holy living
Helps to heal the ground.

Givers shine within the giving
Luminous around.

Selflessness gives joy to mortals
And integrity,
Widening the spirit's portals
Lends immensity.

## BABY GIRL

Her contribution to mankind
Like honeysuckle, is confined
To exudation of a sense
Of fragrance and of innocence.

## ST. PAUL'S CATHEDRAL

St. Paul's Cathedral just today
Is filled with mighty choirs and throngs,
Assembling that the world might pay
The tributes of its prayers and songs
Before Sir Winston Churchill's bier,
And from a distance we grieve here.

## THE BURNING BUSH

The priest of Midian, Jethro, had great flocks
Which he entrusted to his son-in-law,
The youthful Moses, who beneath the rocks
Of Horeb, lofty Sinai, felt awe
Creep over him as there stood in the clear
A burning bush, light boughed, blaze leaved, fire plumed,
Angel inhabited, enkindling fear
Within him as the bush was not consumed.
He stood there thinking of the palace days,

## The Burning Bush

Of Pharaoh's daughter, and a Nile man's bier,
Of hasty flight, of Midian and its ways,
Then heard a voice say, "Moses, come not near,
So sacred is the ground. Put off your shoes.
Your feet are holy, even they have been
Formed from the ground of Being, and unloose
Your sandals that not one thing be between
The ground and dedicated man. Your mind
Let find repose in that I am your God,
Revealed and yet concealed lest you be blind,
Made known this hushed, this beauteous period."
There stood the chosen man and he who chose
This ark-in-bullrush, once-protected child
The one to hear, the other to disclose
The destiny of man unreconciled
To bondage for himself or for the Jews.
"I will send you to Pharaoh. You shall see
My people out, proclaiming bold the news
That Being wills that beings shall be free."
Astonished, Moses, dreading such a plan
Attempted to excuse himself in vain,
But Deity was adamant, and man
Was silent by a bush upon a plain.

## WHAT ELSE?

A minister in the church
Whether occupying the lowliest
Appointment in the conference,
Or the loftiest seat,
Who, under the bludgeonings of opposition
Or of disappointment can remain
Humble and sweet in his soul,
Is still God's man,
And what else could conceivably matter?

*Aldersgate Methodist Church, 4601 Benton Blvd.,*
*Kansas City, Missouri*

## SLEET

Awakening at three o'clock one night
I watched a Sunday morning shower of sleet,
While looking from the bedroom toward a light
Suspended on its pole above the street.
As it drove down upon a bed of snow,
The sleet obscured the light with mist-like haze
And turned the limbs of trees which caught the glow
To chandeliers of crystal through the glaze.
I slept again and with the breaking dawn
Awakened to a whiteness everywhere
Which lent a sense of wonder to the lawn
And put a crispness in the winter air.
The church bus could not run and very few
Attended services at Aldersgate,
But the excitement outdoors with the new
White crusted drifts brought joys to compensate.
When Monday came and news was noised about
There was no school, our children laughed aloud.

66

The streets were ice; no busses could get out.
Instead a sled, on paths its runners plowed
Carried our truant daughters down the hill
Behind the house, each taking turn to ride,
While like a painting framed in window sill
Their parents watched their pleasure from inside.
To love variety requires a mind
Which welcomes all the seasons that appear
And knows each wild, if inconvenient, kind
Of weather lends a richness to the year.

## RECONCILIATION

Let reconciliation lift the pall
Of darkness that has covered us so long.
Let thaw the frozen snowfields, and let all
Volcanoes start erupting with a song.
Let loose the fires impounded from of old.
Let icebound rivers of dead joys begin
To moisten at the edges, and the cold,
Hard surfaces grow fluid-like again.
Let sound the rush, the sweeping, and the roar
Of cataracting rivers of delight,
As once lost joys they happily restore,
And blessed day leaps from the gloom of night.
Then you shall be loved with a joy more vast,
As former bliss is eclipsed by the last.

## I LOVE YOU TOO MUCH TO LOVE
## YOU TOO MUCH

I love you too much to love you too much,
Though lonely you are, as lonely am I,
Nor would I, selfish, hold you in the clutch

Of scheming friendship's fond monoply,
Save when I have a fear that at your side
I may not sit, nor longer have a place
Where beauty that no innocence can hide
Is seen upon a cherished human face.
Oh then I ask that one thing you will do,
Be patient, and let gentle be your touch
If one who brings his loneliness to you
Should seem, dear heart, to love you much too much.
For I would love as angels do in spheres
Unmoved by space, time, passions, or the years.

## TO CHARLES PERRY GODBEY

I scarce can think of anything to write
And you have made me promise that each day
Shall see some verses made before the night
Has thrown the opportunity away.
By telepathic wisdom send me aid,
Your cogitations concentrate this way
To help me write a sonnet which, when made
Will please your taste and thus fulfill the day.
The books that fail in content we disdain,
The art that shows us nothing leaves a lack,
As no one hates his brother without pain,
And he cannot see God, whose heart is black.
Let me be loving, sensitive, and true
That what I write may make some sense to you.

## NINETEEN SEVENTY-EIGHT

Nineteen Seventy-eight
Arrives with hopes renewed
Which now we reinstate
Across the interlude.

Once more I have resolved
To publish what I write
And find the key involved
To bring a book to light.

And like a raging fire
Combustive in intent
The zeal of this desire
Shall see a book in print.

## TO DAWN

Of all my teachers, you, Dawn, first-born soul,
I thank the most for lessons you have taught
And for the infant helplessness which brought
Me humbly to my first parental role.
I stretched you out upon me, closely pressed,
Your feet reached hardly lower than my waist
When you were tiny, fair, and angel-faced,
Asleep but rising with my breathing chest.
I showed you pictures long before you read,
My hobby books your first curriculum.
The names of all the fowls in Christendom
You learned while watching pictures in my bed.
But now we switch the roles we played before,
And I, in silence, listen and adore.

## PRAYER OF THE HUNTED DEER

Deliver us from evil and from death;
We are thy hunted deer, and out of breath
We pant for rest and for a waterbrook.
We vainly race to find a shaded nook
Where we might hide from the pursuing hounds.

We long for respite from the chilling sounds,
The burning breath that makes the fever soar
Within our throbbing lathered sides, this roar
That tortures the already stricken brain.
Preserve our lives and take us back again.
Rescue our world. Heal our disease. Preserve
Us from destruction which we may deserve.
Lest our last century be the twentieth,
O snatch us from the jaws of snapping death.

## A KIND PATERNITY

There is a cosmic happiness in the soul
Akin to sweet October's hastening fall
Of leaves. Then as the somber seasons roll,
And one remembers other autumns all
Sedately moving toward eternity,
He thinks of God and Time's swift flowing stream.
One then can trace a kind Paternity
Whose purposes pervade man's purest dream.

## OUR PATHWAY

I owe the world a song
For all of life is singing
And gladness is not wrong
For one so richly bringing
A heart with praise to you,
Our God, who gave us breath,
And makes our pathway through
Life here, and after death.

## CAMP GALILEE REVISITED

I took a thoughtful walk today
Into a ball field rank with hay
And sought out where its bases lodged
Grown up with weeds and camouflaged.
At last was found a large stone, propped
Upon a mound and overtopped
By daisies, hidden in the field.
I knew then that a search would yield
The outline of each infield stone
And so soon found myself alone
Upon the central mound where I
Last year had watched the balls sail by.
In reverie I stood at home
Within this small world's hippodrome
And from its exaltation brought
Remembered things from realms of thought.
I was a counselor of youths
Who sandwiched exercise with truths
And since they sought a place for ball
I led them to this place where all
Could take the field and try to rise
Through competition's enterprise
To some distinction in the game,
Or best, at camp, some gleam of fame.
Today alone in thought I stood
Upon this spot where once my brood
Of restless lads with eager feet
Played here in summer sun and heat.
I thought of how the seasons rolled
From summer's heat to autumn's cold,
Of how the snow lay deep in piles
Across the intervening miles

During my absence from this place.
Now with the spring's recurring grace
Except for changes time entails
And hikers missed along the trails
And sessions we cannot restore,
The camp is as it was before.
And though one misses with regret
The faces he cannot forget,
Yet still because of years outgrown
A richness clings to leaf and stone.

## THE GREATEST COMPLIMENT

The greatest compliment
Which a human being
Ever paid another human being
In the history of the world
Was the subconscious tribute
Which Jesus paid to Joseph
When, in teaching his disciples to pray,
He began by saying:
"Our Father . . . ."

## A TEENAGE PROTEST AGAINST
## RELIGIOUS SKEPTICISM

We hope we find not through the years
That man is but a force of brain.
We trust we do not strive in vain
When seeking God with earnest tears.

We trust we are not gript for naught
In struggling against the sway of death
Like Paul who felt the glowing breath
When with Ephesian beasts he fought.

*A Teenage Protest Against Religious Skepticism*

Let science never prove that we
Are but clay forms of clever mold
Lest life itself and science hold
No more of interest for me!

Should wise men ever count the beast
And man alike in form and fate,
Then rise, my soul, nor linger late,
For thou canst sing thy songs at least.

## MY LOVE IS LIKE THE MOUNTAIN TOP

My love is like the mountain top
Communing with the blue;
Before its peak I, silent, stop
To breathe a prayer for you.
For this great rugged monument
Is surely from above
The symbol of a spirit sent
And of a glorious love.

## TRUE LOVE IS LIKE THE MIDNIGHT AIR

True love is like the midnight air
Where not a breeze may start,
When like a deep red rose and fair
Affection fills the heart.
Love's breath against the cheek does blow
Like the rose's scent at night
That makes the midnight breeze aglow
With strange and hidden light.

O fairest loves and dearest souls
How often memory places
Her fingers well upon the scrolls
Where first we saw your faces.

In oneness as in youthful days
May lovers ever be
Through life and death and fields of praise
Beside an emerald sea.

## FOX

This morning looking from the door
To watch the glow of daylight pour
Across the woods that edge our lawn,
I saw a fox against the dawn.

He walked out where the okra grows,
On past tomato plants in rows
Toward the denser undergrowth
Where larger elms lend shade to both.

He sought a meal of hen, but mine
Were housed so that he could not dine,
And as the red one vainly crept
Our cocks and hens securely slept.

But we within the city's bounds
Were glad that in escape of hounds
So wild a creature could contrive
To walk in beauty still alive.

## AMERICAN BICENTENNIAL

To celebrate our land of birth,
Great America's loved sweet earth,
We sift through fingers or plowshare
Its cherished soil, now unaware
But once the astonishment of Viking chiefs,
Then seen by Columbus on Indian reefs,

## American Bicentennial

Traversed by Spaniards from anchored fleet,
Touched by their bare or sandalled feet,
Land of the pilgrim and Indian host
And sermons of fire and the Holy Ghost,
Land grown restless with English rule,
Provoking the wrath of a royal fool
Until both patriots and redcoats cast
Their lots, returning the rifle's blast;
Land that brought forth Washington,
Dominant, tenacious, fearless son,
Whose force of character helped to weld
A state the people's will upheld.
Beautiful land, you became embroiled
In strife where human slaves had toiled
And a million soldiers, hurt or dead,
Paid for our unity where they bled.
Vast, brooding Lincoln, sweet in soul,
Keeping his course while the war drums roll,
Stamping his greatness with strong, firm hands,
Sent forth a legend across the land.
Great holy soil, you sent your might
Into the Kaiser's lines to fight,
Resisting ambition's cruel outrage
And rescued the world from vassalage.
Another anguish, the Nazi wall
Of steel and fire brought fear to all
And death to millions in its path
Till it encountered the new world's wrath.
That wrath prevailed, a world was saved
By those who never were enslaved,
And now our efforts shall not cease
To heal a world through powers of peace.

## THE YOUNG GEORGE WASHINGTON

Bold upon the continent unformed
Appeared the archetypal youth,
Rugged, tall, and muscular
Six feet three and a half inches
Towering above the small men of his time,
With character to match his stature.
With powerful legs striding across the land,
Surveying it, enjoying every hour afoot,
Growing into manhood with a will,
He built the strength and health to rule the land.
His auburn hair whose red was later turned
Into a reddish brown was freely blown
By winds out in the wilderness before
A wig of white would hide it from the world,
But that same stubborn jaw and flintlike face,
That countenance of handsome strength, was there.
Graceful in the saddle, he could turn a horse
As no one else among plantation youths,
And riding later, gave men inspiration
As armies moved, and men endured,
The French appeared, a trap was sprung,
And he stood foremost in a world
To which he gave a nation.


## THE HOUSE OF TOMORROW

Kahlil Gibran, a voice from Lebanon,
Has spoken of our children with the thought
That they whom we've begotten aren't our own;
They through us, but not from us, have been brought
Not to the place we choose, for they shall dwell

In the house of tomorrow which we can't visit
Not even in our dreams, and this is well,
For they go to a house more exquisite
Than we can conceive. We will it so
For their dear good, yet feel a wistful ache
In knowing that a part of us must go
Where we cannot, and lose them for their sake.

## CONVERSION

The most important event in the life of the youthful poet after his birth into the world was the religious experience which occurred at age 19, when the parsonage-bred youth moved from his marginal, inherited, religion into a complete dedication which brought an ecstasy of spiritual joy. This poem was written at the age of 19 and no word has been changed.

O God, my soul is all Thine own,
And yearns for only Thee,
And loves Thy name, and Thine alone
Shall ever hope to be.

I love Thy truth, unvarnished, plain;
The world I've left behind.
All compromisers seek in vain
My fellowship to find.

My heart the flaming truth once heard
And straightway with desire
Thy holiness my spirit stirred
And set these bones afire.

Could it be true that Thou could'st claim
One's soul and make it pure?
Could'st purge one's sins, forgive his blame
And make his heaven sure?

O praise Thy name, I brought my need,
Forgetting all beside,
A church profession and a creed,
My future, friends, and pride.

I gave my youthful heart to Thee,
My all, complete, entire.
Thy sweet forgiveness set me free
And brought the sacred fire.

## ACROSS THE VANISHED YEARS (ST. JAMES)

Across the vanished years a sweetness drifts
Down through an orchard northward from a house
With barn and sheds off to the east,
A fence with woods on to the north,
And at the west a graveled road beyond which
Parallel a railroad slices through a gash
West of the front yard oaks that crown the hill.
The scenery of the soul in memory
Outlasts the high walls that protrude
Through trees that are no more;
And that old house so long ago destroyed by fire
Is standing still where flames cannot consume.

The sweetness which like ghostly honeysuckle
Blows across the leap of years
Is of a mother singing at a kitchen stove,
A tall and thoughtful father splitting wood
To help to turn an orchard into pies,
And six who would consume its food and warmth.
One son attended Central College in the north,
Two more were home and helped to fell the trees,
Two little daughters played and kept the house
And helped to tend a tiny boy, the last.

After play in lofts and woods and rock-strewn paths,
They gathered at the table for the grace
Their father said, and for their mother gathered food.

They loved exploring rambling upper halls
And rooms in which they slept, exhausted after play,
Near windows touched by outside branches blowing
From shadowed oak trees keeping watch by night.
These things possessed, we are of them possessed.
We who were theirs, though scattered far,
Still keep the faith and feel the sweetness drifting
Across the vanished years.

## FRAGMENTS: ST. JAMES SUMMER

When I was but a lad our father paused
Between appointments and for eight months dwelt
Upon a farm outside St. James and caused
Our minds to relish what we lived and felt.

Adjacent to the barn some giant oaks
Towered by its roof and in their branches sang
Some feathered singers echoing the croaks
Of pond-based frogs as all the forest rang.

While looking from the barn loft on this scene
We children facing toward the house and yard,
Then felt like kings surveying our demesne
And found in every moment a reward.

Yet even as the concert in the wood
Was at its peak the sun began to wane
And with approaching dusk we understood
That night was stealing over us again.

I well remember how the oak trees swept
Their leafy branches out in shadowed mass
Above the upper chamber where we slept
As they kept guard to watch the night hours pass.

## A TOILER IN THE DARST BOTTOMS, DEFIANCE

Out in the bright fields where the golden wheat
Waves in long ripples with the blast of heat
Blown with the wind upon the heads of grain
The harvest worker toils and longs for rain,
Not rain to flatten stalks but rain to halt
The burning and bring clouds across the vault
Of parching sky and add variety
To days of fair and hot satiety.

The toil is not without its own reward
For, turning to the south, the eyes regard
The mighty head of bluffs above the tides
Beneath whose face of rock Missouri glides,
And undulating from this highest peak
On either side the lower bluff lines speak,
Though mute, of peace and permanence and might,
And of the Power of Being, day and night.

When daylight hours are spent, the evening sun
Proclaims without a clock that work is done.
They who have toiled in harvest through the day
Rejoice in going home to love and play.
The weary thighs and backs are healed by rest,
The hungry appetites with food are blest,
And all the deeper hungers satisfied
By God and man, the bridegroom and the bride.

## TO THOSE AT HOME, CHRISTMAS 1933

This piece is copied from a rhymed letter sent by the homesick freshman at M.U. to his parents in early December and, while full of imperfections, it conveyed the love for his family which the writer felt.

Now come the winds of Christmas time,
Now comes the sparkling snow,
And soon the river's flowing rhyme
Shall feel its cadence slow.
Now soon the bluffs, their faces hard
With ice, we'll look upon.
We'll walk the trails we loved toward
The scenes of joy beyond.
United soon we all shall be
For two short weeks of bliss.
My fondest wish would be that we
Could always live like this!
I try to picture now each move
When my stray ship comes late
Some winter's eve to those I love
All gathered at the gate.
How in their midst I'll safe be borne
Beside the old home fire
Where with those hearts from whom I'm torn
I'll be beyond desire.
My stalwart dad at first I'll see
And tell, perhaps, some plan,
And pray the Lord that I might be
At last, like him, a man.
Our blessed mother I'll adore
As I've done in the past;
I'll stand and watch her from the door,

Near her again at last.
No older boy excels in grace
The one I'll sit beside;
My brother, David, holds his place
As my first friend and guide.
Anticipation sets a stage
For conversation's joys
With Howard, the nearest to my age,
On things we did as boys.
For Christmas tales I must make plans
For those whose special realm
Of faeries, bears, and Mexicans
Has Santa at the helm.
The name of Margaret was given
Each boy before his birth,
But then at last she came from Heaven,
The cutest girl on earth.
The next was Martha, poet wreathed,
The picture near complete;
Of all the bards who ever breathed
Not one was half so sweet.
Our little brother, Dick, is dear,
So much so, here's a test;
If one could be the dearest here,
He's more so than the rest.

## CARDINALS

One could scarcely imagine a cloud
Of cardinals in mass
Red in the sky,
Or hearing explosions of loud
Redbird twitter harass
Passersby,

For Nature provides a parity,
One lone crested darling,
Scarlet in song,
Equalling in its rarity
Blackened skies of starling
Or sparrow throng.

## JOHN WESLEY

John Wesley stood upon a knoll
And preached his fiery sermon,
And those in Bristol heard it roll
Like thunder from Mount Hermon.

By twice ten thousand was he heard
And by thousands more around
Who seemed to drink in every word
Like rain on the thirsty ground.

Asked to explain the crowd's desire,
Wesley told them in return,
"I only pray myself on fire
And they come to watch me burn!"

## BIRTHDAY 1966

To celebrate this birthday with a rhyme
I sing of time and times and half a time,
Of time because some steady metronome
Unheard, beats out our muffled march toward home;
Times, speaking with apocalyptic voice
Recount the journey wherein we rejoice,
And half a time for we cannot unveil
Just what our half-completed tasks entail.
When in the mountains, sundown darkness falls,
An afterglow lights up the eastern walls,

For though the sun may sink below our sight,
A backward glimpse reveals the hills are bright.
Our times have now the glow of distant gates
Where ultimate reality awaits.

## TODAY IS MAY SECOND

Today is May second, nineteen seventy-three
Meaning that Mother Davis's Potosi parsonage child,
Who was born on this date on a Sunday, wonders how
She would view him, were she still on earth.
She would be happy to know that he is happy, for he is;
She could be comforted to know that he is loved, for he
        is;
She would be pleased to know that he is well, and he is,
And would see her faith justified in that he has faith,
        which he has,
And would like knowing that he is a man of love,
        for this he is,
And she would see the travail of her soul
        and be satisfied,
And know that over herself and him, death
        has no dominion.

## A POET SEES THE YEAR OUT (1974)

This is December thirty-first and I
Am conscious that the dying year has brought
Few poems to completion, and I ought
To add one more before the month slips by.
In looking over those which I might try
To have preserved, I sometimes have the thought
That these secluded notebooks may have caught

A Poet Sees the Year Out

Some moods with which all could identify.
The poet, Robert Frost, once said that he
Had some six hundred poems he composed
In sixty years of labor, and disclosed
That this was some ten poems annually.
I count my poems, too, at each year's close
And find but few; most of the year is prose!

## DELIGHT

Once on a time as work for church and school
Kept me away from home almost all day,
Delight, our one-and-one-half-year-old girl
So greatly missed her father all day long
That when she heard my footsteps in the hall
She ran, and to her father's arms she leaped
And on my shoulders snuggled her wee head.
My face she patted with her baby hand,
And murmured in her infant happiness
The soft expression, "Happy," learned at home.
While holding her there came the thought to me,
How often must our older natures too
Yearn for a closeness no one quite can give
Who is but human; thus it is ordained.
As said the great Augustine long ago,
Our souls God has created for Himself
And restless must we be without His rest.
We can no more endure without Him near
And still be happy than could my Delight
Find her desire to snuggle on the breast
Of her sire satisfied by being sent
To bed with some poor substituted toy.

85

## FAITH, HOPE, AND LOVE

There is a gentle sweetness in the air;
A haunting sense of loveliness enfolds
The wonders of existence everywhere
When Faith finds charm in all which it beholds.

Where Hope gives life to dullest platitude
Confusion yields to meaning, every place,
And all things wrought with gratitude
Are beautified through an interior grace.

But of all virtues which give life its joy
The greatest, smoothing pathways all must take,
Is being home at last in the employ
Of Love, and doing for another's sake.

## FIRST SNOW (1973)

The noise of wind accompanies the drift
As downward softly floats the first of snows
And winter darkness aggravates the rift
From summer which the icy tempest blows.
Outside a person scarce can stand erect
Upon the ice glazed walks, and glassy street,
And still a certain glory in effect
Has more than compensated for the sleet.
We're still aware, no matter how the scene
Revives old memories, that some must go
On journeys unavoidable that mean
Exposure to the perils of the snow.
Deliverance is given through our trust
That what we pray for, finds us as it must.

## SOMETIMES

This poem written at the age of 18 has not had one word changed from its first writing, and preserves a youth's excessive sadness over an unsuccessful affair of the heart.

Sometimes life's first black bitter draughts
Dye dark with pain my crushing fears;
Sometimes I sit alone with thoughts
That sting too deep for human tears.

Sometimes my heart beholds a face
Too sacred, sweet, and dear to name;
Sometimes its wild romantic grace
Blots out with love, teardrops of pain.

Sometimes I think back on the nights
When in the stars I've seen that soul;
Sometimes my melancholy flights
Of passion near their starry goal.

Sometimes I reel before the brink,
The dark abyss that separates;
Sometimes its drugging deeps I drink
But cannot cross the bar of fates.

## ROBERT CHURCH

A plane cleared the Missouri with a loud
Uprising as it soared into the grey
Oblivion of lostness in a cloud
Of Kansas City fog across the way.
I watched, then gazed through rain and boisterous wind
Toward Trinity Hospital in mid-town
Where Robert Church, who long had been my friend
Lay with life's final curtain closing down.

As through the rain the giant plane soared on,
He left his runway, too, in unseen flight
Into a cloud-obscured and misty dawn
Beyond our help, our knowledge, or our sight.

## THOUGHTS ON WRITING LATE

There seems not much tonight to say,
No content seeking out a way
To thrust itself upon mankind
Embodied from a heated mind.
And I am weary from the day
And rest seems calling me away
From this attempt to vindicate
A day which seeks, if much too late,
To be redeemed from emptiness
By late attempts at word success.
Yet I have learned the power which lies
In daily adding new supplies
To an accumulated mass
When one allows no day to pass
Without enlarging, as one ought,
The total of one's written thought.
Our adding daily each day's lines
To those of yesterday defines
In time some literary feat,
Or else, at least, a task complete.

# BIOGRAPHICAL NOTES

Phil Freund photo

*Harry Benoist Davis, 1981*

For those who might be interested in knowing more about the circumstances behind this book, these notes are possibly of some interest.

Harry Benoist Davis, son of Reverend David Robertson and Martha Benoist Davis, was born May 2, 1915 in the Methodist parsonage at Potosi, Missouri. He subsequently lived in Lowndes, Whitewater, Deslodge, Salem, Eureka, Mountain Grove, Licking, Saint James, Hallsville and Defiance, all in Missouri. From Defiance he entered the University of Missouri at Columbia and obtained his A.B. in 1937. He taught at Mount Zion Bible College, Ava, Missouri and at the Kansas City College and Bible School in Kansas City. He pastored the Rayville Methodist Circuit in 1940 and Institutional Methodist Church in Kansas City in 1942.

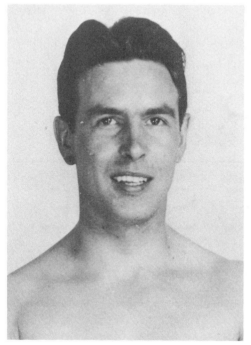

*Harry Davis, at YMCA Gym, 1944*

After earning an M.A. in teaching English at the University of Kansas City in 1944 and a Divinity degree (M.Div.) at Garrett Theological Seminary of Northwestern University in 1946, he pastored the Dawn-Liberty Methodist Circuit in 1945-46 and the Galt Circuit in 1946-47 where the Ora Holts and daughter, Marvis, were members. Davis then took the Glasgow, Missouri, Methodist pastorate (1947-49) and the Winnwood, North Kansas City, Methodist Church (1949-52) where he was the founding pastor of the new Northmoor Methodist Church.

In 1952 he was appointed to the Marsh Avenue

Methodist pastorate in Kansas City where he gathered a new congregation together and started Kansas City Countryside Methodist Church, one of the city's finest. He also pastored the Sugar Creek church during this period. Pastorates followed at Slater in 1958-60 (where he wrote *The Emerald Valley*) and Oak Grove, in 1960-65 (*Saint James* and *Jesse Hall*).

In 1955 occurred an event which ranks with his birth and a spiritual experience at age 19 as one of the three most important events of his life: his marriage to Marvis Holt. Marvis was a fourth grade teacher at Bethany, Missouri, a graduate of Kirksville State College and the daughter of the Holts of Galt.

This marriage was performed at the Fairview Church north of Galt by the groom's father, Rev. D. R. Davis, who was then in his eighties. It led to the six events which alone would rank with the first three in importance in the poet-pastor's life: the births of the Davis daughters. Dawn (1956) and Melody (1957) were born in Independence during the Marsh Avenue pastorate, Delight (1959) at Marshall during the Slater assignment, Miracle (1960) and Heather (1963—the year father D. R. Davis passed) while the family lived at Oak Grove, and Heidi (1968) during the Aldersgate years. Mother Davis died in 1961. She and father Davis are buried at Chillicothe, Missouri, their last home.

From Oak Grove the family moved to the Cambridge Street home in Kansas City, parsonage of the imposing Aldersgate Methodist Church, from which the writer pastored the Aldersgate congregation and wrote his Cambridge Street poems. The ten years at this church (1965-75) were among the happiest, spent with a growing family, doing the work of the church and of the books. Later assignments included the United Methodist churches, Faith, College Heights, and Mount Calvary, the relocated and renamed Marsh Avenue congregation to which the writer returned in 1980 and enjoys the affection of a loving and twice-served congregation.

The appearance of *Songs Along the Missouri* ranks among the ten most important events in the poet's life, if the grandchildren list under their mother's headings, as the writer's beloved siblings, are considered as belonging to the event of birth into the Benoist-Davis family. This book could not have been published without the loving assistance of the author's daughter, Dawn Davis Linnabery, of Irving, Texas, who typed the manuscript and urged its publication, Reginald D. Woodcock of Pennsylvania whose encouragement led to the decision to have the book printed, and the expert planning and enthusiasm of a great publisher, Arthur E. Lowell.

The author's lifelong and beloved friend, Harold B. Whaley, long the head librarian at the Unity School of Christianity, first typed and mimeographed *The Emerald Valley*. The writer's sister and twin poet, Margaret Davis Owen, put *Saint James* into a mimeographed book. Margaret, five years younger than her brother, and her yet-younger sister, Martha Davis Ware, share their brother's interest in literature and are both exquisite poets.

Finally, the love and inspiration of Marvis and all the daughters, each one a gifted and wonderful person, are behind the writing, providing through their faith the treasures of the spirit necessary to a poet.